M. E. Church South

New Orleans Cook Book

M. E. Church South

New Orleans Cook Book

ISBN/EAN: 9783744790024

Printed in Europe, USA, Canada, Australia, Japan

Cover: Foto ©Lupo / pixelio.de

More available books at **www.hansebooks.com**

New Orleans Cook Book

————BY THE— — -

Womans Parsonage

—— ——AND ————

Home Mission Society,

————OF- ——— —

Parker Memorial

M. E. CHURCH SOUTH.

1898.

—— —— ——

OFFICERS

President.................MRS. J. W. WILKINSON.
Vice-President.....................MRS. L. RIGGS.
Secretary............. ...MRS. J. W. BILLINGTON.
Treasurer....... .. . . MISS C. MITCHELL.

PREFACE.

"Man may live without books.
    What is knowledge but grieving?
He may live without hope.
    What is hope but deceiving?
He may live without love,
    What is passion but pining?
But where is the man that can live without dining?"

The promoters of this modest enterprise hesitate to claim for it that it fills a long felt want; there are other cook books containing vastly more information in which the resources and products of the Frigid Zone and the Tropics are drawn on for the purpose of whetting the human appetite.

The sphere of this little book is more limited, but we feel that it will appeal with great force to its limited circle, for it is especially adapted to their wants—the ingredients called for in the recipes given are always to be had in season in our own markets, and many of the appetizing dishes for which New Orleans and Louisiana are noted, are herein described.

It has not been the aim in compiling these recipes, to tell all we know, or all that our friends know, but out of the generous responses to our requests for "two or three of your very best," we have selected these as the "best of the best." Very few, if any, are original—many have been tried and tested by the mothers and grandmothers of the donors, while others are more modern--thoroughly "up-to-date;" but each recipe carries the enthusiastic recommendation of her whose name is subscribed thereto, and one has but to read over these names to be convinced that we are not too optimistic in expressing the belief that this collection will please all who make use of it.

"Here is bread, which strengthens men's hearts,
and therefore is called "The Staff of Life."

Graham Bread.

Made with equal parts of Graham and white flour. Bake and treat as you would ordinary white bread. The adding of white flour to the Graham prevents the bread from drying up. MISS COCKER.

Graham Bread.

3 pints Graham flour, 1 pint white flour, 1 cup yeast, ½ cup molasses, 1' teaspoonful salt mix with lukewarm water as stiff as you can, stir with a spoon. Let it rise over night and bake in a moderately hot oven. MISS COCKER.

Light Rolls.

Boil one pint of whey, pour on to a half tablespoonful of flour, let stand until cool, then stir into it the yeast, (either yeast cake or compressed,) add flour sufficient to make a stiff batter, and beat half an hour; allow about four hours to rise, then sift the flour, pour into it this batter, add four tablespoonsful of lard, one teaspoonful of sugar, one egg also salt, make out into rolls and when sufficiently raised, bake in hot oven. MRS. W. W. CARRÈ.

Dropped Corn Bread.

One pint of fine white corn meal, thoroughly scalded with boiling water; when cool, add two eggs well beaten; salt to taste, and thin it with sufficient milk to make it drop from spoon (say about half a cup).

Mrs. W. W. Carrè.

Thomas Bread.

One tumbler sweet milk; two eggs, well beaten; two even tablespoonsful sugar; two even tablespoonsful of melted butter; flour until it makes a stiff batter; desertspoonful of Dixie Baking Powder. Mrs. Alma S. Wynn.

BISCUIT.

One quart of flour, one heaping tablespoonful of lard, one teaspoonful of salt, three teaspoonfuls ol Dixie baking powder and sweet milk enough to make a soft dough. Sift the flour, baking powder and salt together three times. (Leave a little of the flour in sifter for the board), sift the flour into the tray or bowl, then put the spoonful of lard in the centre, and mix with the milk, using a large spoon and stirring the dough as little as possible; have the dough as soft as can be handled or rolled out. Roll thin and cut with biscuit cutter, bake at once in a very hot oven.

Mrs. Minnie M. Wilkinson.

Beaten Biscuit.

One quart of flour, one tablespoonful of lard, one good teaspoonful of salt, and sweet milk sufficient to make a stiff dough. Beat long and well, or better still, roll through a dough kneader until the dough blisters and pops.

Mrs. W. H. LaPrade, Shreveport, La.

Graham Bread.

One cake compressed yeast; three quarts of Graham flour; one kitchen spoonful of lard; one large cup of brown sugar; one tablespoon of salt; mix well the lard, sugar and salt into the flour before putting in your yeast which should be well dissolved in *cold* water; if set by eight in the morning, will be ready to make into loaves by three in the afternoon.   Mrs. H. J. Mullen.

Corn Meal Bread.

One pint of corn meal; one teaspoon of salt; two large tablespoons of hot rice; one or two eggs, beat together; pour on just enough boiling water to make a thick mush; form it into a round cake in a pie-plate, being careful to not let it get cold; then bake until there is a good crust bottom and top; don't use fine meal.

Corn Meal Cakes.

One pound of sugar; half pound butter; one nutmeg; one pound of meal; four eggs; one cupful of flour; after sifting the meal take out a cupful of meal and put into the cupful of flour; beat up with other ingredients, and drop from a spoon on greased pans and cook in quick oven.

                    Miss Mary Wilkinson.

Breakfast and Tea Cakes.

JOHNNY CAKES.

Two cups of Indian meal in your mixing dish, add one pint of sour milk or butter-milk, a spoonful of cream or butter; beat well together and add a cup full of flour, with a teaspoon of soda sifted through it. Bake in a quick oven and serve hot for breakfast.   MISS MARY WERLEIN.

Buckwheat Cakes.

Two cups buckwheat flour, one cup wheat flour, four teaspoons Dixie baking powder, one teaspoon salt, one tablespoon sugar, mix altogether and add sufficient sweet milk or water to make a soft batter. Bake on griddle at once.   MRS. S. F. G.

Graham Gems.

Three pints of Graham flour, one small cup of brown sugar, 1 teaspoon of salt, two scant teaspoons of Dixie baking powder, one tablespoon of lard, make dough much softer than for ordinary biscuits, bake in a quick oven.
     MRS. H. J. MULLEN.

Rice Cakes.

One cup cold boiled rice, one pint of flour, 1 teaspoon of salt, two eggs well beaten, milk to make a thick batter. Fry—   MRS. M. WALKER.

MUFFINS.

Two cups of flour, two heaping teaspoonsful Dixie baking powder, three heaping teaspoonsful of sugar, one tablespoonful butter. Work the butter well into the mixture with a spoon, add ¾ of a cup of cold water, and one egg well beaten. Fill the moulds and bake in hot oven.

Mrs. W. H. Belt.

Flannel Cakes.

Sift together 1½ pints of flour, one tablespoonful brown sugar, a little salt, add two beaten eggs, one pint of miik, heat into a smooth thin batter. Bake on hot griddle to a rich brown. Miss M. Keen.

French Rolls.

One quart flour, two ounces butter, a little salt well rubbed together, one well beaten egg, ½ compressed yeast cake dissolved in luke warm milk, add as much sweet milk as required to make a stiff batter, beat well and set to rise. When light, roll out thin, cut into gems, brush edges with butter, fold them over, place a little distance apart in the pan. Let stand a while to rise again and bake.

Mrs. Heck.

Light Flour Puffs for Breakfast.

Take a tumbler of sifted flour, a tumbler of milk and two eggs. Put a spoonful of Dixie yeast powder in the flour before sifting, beat eggs (up) separately. Mix together and add a teaspoonful of melted butter or lard just before baking in little fancy pans. Put salt in the flour with the yeast powder and then bake as quickly as you can. Mrs. J. T. Sawyer.

Doughnuts, Cookies, Ginger Bread

DOUGHNUTS.

One cup sour milk, 1½ cups sugar, one egg, one table-spoon melted lard, ¼ teaspoon baking soda, flavor to taste, flour sufficient to roll out; and fry in hot lard.

Mrs. Alice M. Zable.

GINGERBREAD.

A cupful each of sour cream and nice molasses. A level teaspoonful and a half of soda a teaspoonful each of salt and ginger, add flour to make a little thicker than griddle cakes. Bake in eight in a sheet.

Miss Mary Werlein.

Soft Cookies.

One heaping cup butter, 1½ cups sugar, 3 eggs beaten separately, 3 tablespoons sour milk, 1 small teaspoon of soda, and as little flour as will make them stiff enough to roll. Sprinkle with sugar and grated nutmeg before cutting, pass over roller, cut and bake a light brown.

COOKIES.

Two cups sugar, 1 cup butter, ¾ cup sweet milk, 2 eggs, 5 cups flour, 2 teaspoons Dixie yeast powder. Roll thin and bake quickly.

Mrs. S. F. G.

Graham Crackers.

Two cups Graham flour, 1 cup white flour, ½ cup sugar ½ cup butter, 1 egg, salt to taste. Roll and bake in a quick oven.

Miss Cocker.

Soft Ginger Bread.

3 cups flour, ½ cup milk, ½ cup lard, ½ cup New Orleans molasses, 1 teaspoonful soda, 2 eggs, 1 teaspoonful of ginger. Beat the yolk of the eggs and the lard together, then add the milk, soda, molasses, ginger and flour, then beat the whites to a stiff froth and add them carefully. Bake in a moderate oven ¾ of an hour.

Miss Cocker.

Thin Rich Cookies.

1 cup butter, 1 cup sugar, 3 eggs, all beaten together to a cream, use just enough flour to mix and roll thin.

Mrs. S. F. G.

Good Cookies.

2 cups of sugar, 1 cup of butter, 3 cups of flour, 1 cup of sour cream or milk, 3 eggs, 1 teaspoon of soda. Mix soft, roll thin, sift granulated sugar over them, and gently roll it in.

Mrs. P. R. Baldwin, Biloxi, Miss.

Dr. A. G. BOWMAN,

SOUPS.

Cream of Tomato Soup.

One pint can of tomatoes, one pint of fresh sweet milk, half teaspoon of soda, one spoon butter, two tablespoons of rolled cracker crumbs. Place over fire the tomatoes and stew till soft, add soda and stir till effervescence ceases. Strain it so no seeds remain, set over the fire again and add a pint of hot milk, season with salt and pepper and put in the cracker crumbs. Serve very hot.

Green Pea Soup.

One pint of sweet milk, one spoon of butter, two table-spoons of rolled cracker crumbs. Place over the fire the peas in a little water and stew till soft, add the hot milk and butter with a small spoonful of sugar or condensed milk, season with salt and pepper and put in the cracker crumbs and serve.

Mrs. A. C. King.

Vermicelli Soup.

One pound vermicelli boiled half hour, salt and pepper to taste, add as much water as needed. Beat the yolk of one egg well, and stir in as the soup is poured up.

Mrs. Lucie Menard.

Beef Soup.

Take a ten cents brisket or soup bone, put it into a pot of water and let boil during breakfast. When it is time to start dinner, cut or chop up one turnip, one carrot, one onion, a few sprigs of parsley and chillots, and add to soup. Just before serving, thicken it with tablespoon of flour mixed with water, season to taste with salt and pepper.
Miss Mary Wilkinson.

Oyster Soup.

Put the liquor which drains from 3 dozen oysters into a marbleized sauce pan. Let it heat and skim thoroughly, then add a teaspoon of finely chopped onions and parsley, a sprig of thyme, also a heaping tablespoon of butter, mixed with a teaspoon of flour, salt and pepper to taste, add ½ dozen cloves and spice. Put in oysters last, let ting them boil two minutes. Have warm, a pint of fresh milk, which add just before dishing.
Mrs. S. S. Keener.

Mock Turtle Soup.

1 large spoon of lard, 1 of flour browned together, add 1 pound of beef chopped small, ½ can tomatoes, 6 whole alspice, salt and pepper to taste, add 3 quarts water and simmer until beef is tender. Chop 2 hard boiled eggs in the tureen, pour soup on, squeeze in the juice of half a lemon, and slice in the other half.
Mrs. G. P. Work.

Apple Soup.

Peel and core six apples, cut them up and boil them well in 8 cups of water, boil till tender, strain through a colender; return to pot, boil up again with a little cinnamon bark, a piece of lemon peeling and sugar to taste, and a tiny bit of salt and serve either hot or cold.

Prune Soup.

½ pound of prunes, wash them well, add 8 cups of water and boil, add a piece of cinnamon, lemon peeling, when it begins to boil, 1 tablespoon sago and sugar to taste, boil altogether one hour. Serve either hot or cold.

Milk Soup.

Add to 4 cups of milk, 2 cups of water, a small piece of cinnamon, a piece of lemon peeling, a teaspoonful of butter. When boiling add a little salt and a tablespoonful of sago, boil until clear.

Blackberry Soup.

Take 2 cups of berries, and boil with 8 cups of water at least half an hour. Strain and return the juice to the fire. When boiling add a tablespoonful of sago, a piece of lemon peeling and cinnamon and sugar to taste.

Mrs. J. Cohen.

Simple Tomato Soup.

Add to 1 pint of tomatoes, 1 pint of water, a bay leaf, ¼ teaspoon of celery seed; rub together 2 tablespoons of butter and 2 of flour, stir in the first mixture and cook for 5 minutes, strain, reheat and serve.

Mrs. F. A. Dicks.

Oyster Gumbo Fele.

Take four dozen oysters and strain off the liquor through a seive. Then take one tablespoonful of lard, one of flour and mince, one small onion very fine. Put the lard in pan and when hot add the flour and onion, and fry very brown, then fry the oysters for two or three minutes. Put your liquor on, and boil and skim, adding enough water to make the quantity of soup required. Add parsley, red pepper and salt to taste. Then put in the oysters, and when it comes to a boil, mix one heaping teaspoonful of Felé in a little cold water. Let it cook two minutes and send to the table.

Mrs. S. Henderson.

Chicken Gumbo.

Fry to a light brown a small sized chicken, then add to it a medium sized onion and fry. Add a tablespoon of flour and brown all together, then 'add a pint of boiling water. Have ready a quart of tender okra that has been cut up in thin cross-wise slices, put in the okra and two large tomatoes that have been peeled, and let all cook for one hour or more. When nearly done add corn cut from two ears. Salt and red pepper to suit the taste.

Tchoupitoulas Mission.

GUMBO.

Take a piece of veal, fry brown; also small pieces of ham; fry green okra until ropy; mix altogether with a can of tomatoes and put into a four quart sauce pan or pot with two or three pints of water; cook slowly; adding water gradually to get the required consistency. Pick shrimp and put in while cooking. Season with salt and (liberally) red pepper.

Miss R. Caywood.

Crab Gumbo.

1 can of tomatoes, 1 dozen okra, 1 onion cut fine, 1 tablespoonful of lard. Into the hot lard, sift 2 tablespoonsful of flour, stir until brown. Then put in the tomatoes, okra and onion; to this add about 1 quart and a half of boiling water; let cook until done. Put 1 dozen crabs in boiling water, then remove the top shell, and clean thoroughly, put into the gumbo, and let boil 15 or 20 minutes.

Mrs. Pierce.

Oysters and Crabs

Stuffed Oysters.

4 dozen small oysters, 24 soda crackers soaked in the liquor of the oysters. Chop oysters fine and season with onion, thyme, parsley, etc. Have skillet hot, take one large spoon of lard, and put the mixture in skillet. Add 2 well beaten eggs and 1 large spoon of butter. Cook until done. Have ready 1 dozen shells; fill with mixture, sprinkle with cracker dust. Put in oven and brown.

MRS. C. V. UNSWORTH.

Scollopped Oysters.

¼ cup butter, 1 cup cracker crumbs, 1 dozen oysters, pepper and salt to taste, mix butter and cracker crumbs together, sprinkle ¼ of the crumbs in a bowl, then ½ of the oysters, seasoned, then add rest of crumbs, then the oysters and bake. MRS. A. F. G.

Stuffed Crabs.

Boil your hard crabs and take out the meat. Put a little lard in a frying pan to which add soaked bread and chopped onions. After cooking a little take it up and add an egg, butter, salt and pepper. Clean the shells and fill them with the mixture and put some bread crumbs or crackers over the top and brown in a hot oven.

MRS. H. HAAG.

Fabacher Oyster Patties.

First boil the oysters and set to one side. Cut green onions and brown well with butter and, a tablespoonful of flour. When well stirred together, add a pint of oyster water and the yolks of 3 eggs, ½ lemon. Season to taste with salt and peper. Add oysters and stew all together one-half hour. Then put the fricassee into patties.

SHELLS.

Roll out a nice puff paste thin; cut out with a glass or cookey-cutter, and with a wine glass or smaller cutter, cut out the centre of two out of three; lay the rings thus made on the third and bake at once. If the cutters are dipped in hot water, the edges of the patties will rise much higher and smoother when baking.

MRS. ALMA S. WYNN.

Fried Hard Shell Crabs.

Take six crabs and scald them to kill them. Then clean, break the ends of the claws, salt and pepper. Crush the hard shell a little, roll in corn meal, or in beaten egg, then roll in flour or meal, and fry in hot grease until brown on both sides.

MISS CARRIE LEVY.

Oyster Patties.

Line a small patty pan with puff paste, and bake a light brown; when done, fill with oysters already stewed. The patties should be served and eaten as soon as prepared

MRS. OLIVER.

Oyster Toast.

A nice little dish for a luncheon or late supper. Scald a quart of oysters in their own liquor, take them out and pound or chop them to a paste; add a little cream or fresh butter, and some pepper and salt. Get ready some thin slices of toast moistened with boiling water; and spread with fresh butter; then spread over the butter the oyster paste. Put a thin slice of fresh cut lemon on each piece, and lay parsley on the platter. Serve this hot or it will not be good.

Mrs. J. T. Sawyer,

Oyster Pie.

Three dozen oysters, 1 tablespoonful of butter, 1 teaspoonful of flour, 1 onion, a little parsley, salt and pepper. Brown the flour, fry the onion and add the oyster liquor, salt, pepper, parsley, and last, the oysters. Cook a few minutes and put into a large baking pan into which has been put a short pie crust. Put another crust on top and bake.

French Cook.

Stuffed Crabs.

Boil 1 dozen crabs for about twenty minutes, pick the meat from the shells. Take 1 large onion and fry in hot lard until soft. Soak some stale bread and squeeze tight, add a cupful of the bread, 2 eggs, pepper and salt, chop parsley; now take from the fire and add the crab-meat, mix well, have the shells washed and dried and fill with the stuffing. Sprinkle toasted bread crumbs on top of each one, and put them in the oven and bake about ten minutes.

Mrs. Briggs.

Fried Oysters.

A LA BATTLESHIP MAINE.

Take large oysters from their own liquor put into a thickly folded napkin to dry them; then make hot an ounce each of butter and lard in a thick bottomed frying pan. Season the oysters with pepper and salt, then dip each one into egg and cracker crumbs rolled fine, until it will take up no more. Place them in the hot grease and fry them a delicate brown, turning them on both sides by sliding a broad bladed knife under them. Serve crisp and hot.

Mrs. A. C. King.

FISH

"Master, I marvel how the fishes live in the sea!
Why as men do a'land; the great ones eat up the little ones "

To test fish when cooking, pass a knife along a bone and if it is done, the fish will separate easily. Remove the moment it is done, or it will become insipid. In boiling a fish always plunge it into boiling water and then set where it will simmer gently until done. Garnishes tor fish are parsley, sliced beets and lemon.

COURTBOUILLION.

Take sliced red fish or snapper. Fry each piece brown, make a brown gravy with flour, tomatoes, bay-leaves, a slice of lemon, some spice. Cook the fried fish for half an hour in the gravy and serve. Miss R. Caywood.

Baked Red Fish.

For one large fish, take 1 cup water and 1 can tomatoes, bay leaves, 1 tablespoon of butter, salt and pepper to suit taste and baste well while baking.
Mrs. H. W. Knickerbocker.

To Fry Fresh Herring.

Remove scales, clean, wash and dry; after salting them put in a dish with beaten eggs, turn in powdered toast and fry in butter till brown. Mrs. J. B. A. Ahrens.

Boiled Fish.

Clean thoroughly a large red fish or sheephead. Put into a pot of boiling water, 1 large onion, 1 large head of garlic, 2 large carrots, 1 lemon sliced fine, bay leaves, celery, parsley (stems and leaves) salt and pepper, boil until all the vegetables are soft enough to mash with the potato masher. When the water is well seasoned with the vegetables, tie the fish in a towel and place in the boiling water and let boil for half an hour. When done set aside (in the water) to cool. Serve cold with a boiled sauce.

SAUCE.

Boil 2 eggs hard, rub the yolks fine with 2 tablespoons of sweet oil, using drop by drop. Take the white of the eggs, chop fine with parsley, green onions, olives, mix all together with a tablespoon of capers sauce, vinegar, pepper and salt. Put your fish on a platter, garnish with crisp lettuce leaves, on which are thin slices of lemon and radishes. Pour your gravy over it and serve very cold.

Mrs. D. Rosenbaum.

Trout a la Venitienne.

After well-cleaning your trout, make slashes in the back and insert butter rolled in parsley, lemon, thyme, basil, chives, all minced very fine; pour some salad oil over it, and let it lie for half an hour, cover it with bread crumbs and chopped sweet herbs, boil it over a clear fire which is not too quick, and serve it with sauce.

Mrs. J. T. Sawyer.

Lemon Sauce for Fish.

To half a pint of butter sauce, add the juice of a lemon and another lemon sliced; take out the seeds, and let all boil together. This is good with broiled Spanish mackerel or pompano, also with broiled fish.

Mrs. J. T. Sawyer.

Egg Sauce With Lemon.

Boil six eggs; when cold, take off the shells, and slice them into a cup of melted butter; add pepper and salt, and stir constantly while heating. Add the juice of a lemon or vinegar, or catsup, as preferred. This sauce is equally good for broiled fish or poultry.

Mrs. J. T. Sawyer.

Meats and Fowls

Boiled Meats should be put into boiling water at the beginning to preserve its juices. Keep the water boiling constantly or the meat will soak up the water. Remove meat from water as soon as done.

Science of Baking or Roasting Beef.

Put your beef in a very hot oven at first, keeping the temperature at 300° or more for half an hour, then reduce the heat for the remainer of the time to 200°. Baste the meat every 15 minutes. The great heat at first hardens as well as browns the outer surface, this keeps in the juice. But if the high temperature is kept up the roast will be hard and dry all through instead of rare and juicy as it should be.

Mrs. Buchell.

How to Flavor a Tenderloin Steak.

To assure a delicious steak broil a tenderloin and at the same time small bits of round steak which contains a great deal of well flavored juice. Cut the round steak into small bits and squeeze in a lemon squeezer over the tenderloin. By this method you get a delicious juicy steak.

Mrs. Buchell.

Steak Roll.

Beat the steak well, make a dressing of bread crumbs, pepper, salt, onions, sage and celery, fry it a little, then put it on the steak and roll up and tie, put in oven and bake.

MRS MINNIE WILKINSON.

Roast Beef and Yorkshire Pudding.

Rub a rib roast with salt and pepper, and if not very fat, put in pieces of beef suet. On top and around in pan place pieces of suet, and with these drippings baste every ten minutes. Add *no water at all.* For rare beef, allow 15 minutes to the pound; well done, 20 minutes. Within twenty minutes of serving remove roast, pour all the drippings into a can for future use except about two tablespoonsful and into this pour the pudding, made as follows: 3 eggs well beaten together, to this add a pint of sweet milk, 3 rounded tablespoons of flour measured before sifting, and salt and pepper to taste. Cook until set. Cut in squares and serve around roast. This is the real old English roast-beef, and if basted properly, is very delicious.

MRS. FLORENCE E. RUSS.

Broiled Beef Steak.

Flatten it with the broad side of a hatchet and broil upon a buttered *grid-iron* over a good strong fire; lay it upon a hot dish; season with pepper, salt a large spoon of butter and some finely chopped parsley. Serve at once.

MRS. BRIGGS.

Cold Daube.

8 pounds good roast, 1 pound fresh fat pork, 4 pigs feet, 4 calves feet, 2 beeves feet. Put in pan over night cover with vinegar and let soak. Cut the pork in thin slices. Next morning, put red pepper in the slices of the pork, cut slits in the pork and slip in the peppers ; cover with water and boil slowly until boiled down and thoroughly cooked. Cook the calves and pigs feet separately, (remove all the bones) all to pieces and stir altogether while warm. Cool rapidly in a pan or dish from which it can be turned out whole.

MRS. B. S. STORY.

Virginia Brunswick Stew.

3 gallons water, to which add two chickens cut small, 1 pound fat bacon cut small. When the chickens are sufficiently cooked, remove the meat from the bones and return to the water, then add $\frac{1}{2}$ gallon Irish potatoes, boiled and mashed, $1\frac{1}{2}$ pints green corn cut fine, 1 pint butter beans, 1 quart tomatoes peeled, add onions if liked, pepper, salt and butter. When nearly done add one small loaf of bread. When it begins to thicken stir constantly until done, if too thick add more water. When properly made no one can detect any of the ingredients.

L. S. PARKER.

Meat Balls.

Chop fine whatever cold meat you have, fat and lean together; pepper and salt it. 1 chopped onion, 2 slices of bread which have been soaked in milk, 1 egg, mix all together well. Bake in a form.

MRS. M. WALKER.

DAUBE.

Take four or five pounds of beef (off the round), poke holes in it, push small bits of pork fat and garlic into the gashes. Have the lard boiling hot, put in the beef and brown on both sides. Take out of the pot and brown flour and onions; add a pint of boiling water, tomatoes, garlic, spices. Put the beef in the pot and simmer slowly for three hours.

MISS R. CAYWOOD.

DRY HASH.

Chop either soup meat or cold steak very fine, removing all fat and gristle. Boil and mash 3 or 4 potatoes, mix meat and potatoes. Have ready onion chopped fine and fried in butter, mix with meat and potatoes. Make into small cakes after seasoning with salt and pepper. Fry in hot lard very brown.

French Hash.

Cold soup-meat chopped fine, with onion, pepper and salt. Then put mashed potatoes about a half an inch in baking pan, then the chopped meat. well buttered, and so on until it is all in; being careful to have the last layer potatoes. Spread butter over the top, and put it in the oven to brown.

MRS. PIERCE.

Remnants of Soup Meat with Onions.

Cut the meat in thin slices, saturate with salt water, add to the butter or lard a few well chopped onions. When they are brown put in the meat, cover the pan. Turn the meat after frying a while; when both sides are brown remove. Add to the lard a small quantity of water and flour when a thick sauce, put over the meat and serve while hot.

Beefsteak.

When the pan is very hot moisten it with butter. Put in the steak and let fry three or four minutes. Remove to a hot dish add necessary salt and pepper. Saturate both sides with butter, and serve while warm.

MRS. J. B. A. AHRENS.

Chile Con Carne.

Take a pint of cold meat, any kind, or odds and ends of several kinds can be used, cut it into bits a little longer than the end of your finger, add a chopped onion, ½ pint of left over gravy, a cupful of tomatoes, stew gently half an hour. About five minutes before taking off the fire, stir in a saltspoonful of salt and a dessertspoonful of ground Chile pepper.

Fried Chicken with Cream Gravy.

1 young chicken cut in small pieces; put 1 large kitchen spoon of lard in a frying pan and let it get very hot, salt and pepper the chicken and roll each piece in flour; fry in the hot lard until brown and tender; dish it. Rub 1 spoon of flour and 1 of butter together, stir in the gravy with 1 cup sweet milk, stir until thickened, add a little salt and pepper and parsley cut fine, pour over the chicken.

MISS LILLY B. RIGGS.

Fried Chicken.

Cut the chicken into small pieces and wash thoroughly. Have 2 eggs beaten. with a little salt, into which dip the chicken and then into rolled cracker crumbs, and fry in hot lard.

MRS. J. B. A. AHRENS.

Fried Chicken.

Have your chicken well cleaned and salted. Put some butter to brown in large pot, then put in your chicken and fry till light brown on both sides, add a little water and cover pot tight. Baste frequently with the gravy and add water as needed. A young chicken will require at least one hour of cooking before done. Turkey can be prepared the same way, but it will require three hours cooking.

Chicken Fricassee.

Cut tender chicken into small pieces. Put in the pot with sufficient water to cover. Boil until tender. Strain the liquor, take a tablespoon of butter and sufficient flour to make a gravy with the liquid. Put the chicken into this, add either parsley or pepper or any seasoning preferred. Boil a few minutes.

Mrs. J. Cohen.

Rice Dressing With Oysters.

Put 3 cups rice in 2 cups of water over a quick fire, let come to a good boil, then cover closely and cook slow for ½ hour. Put a large spoon of lard in a pan, add one small onion cut fine, 1 tablespoon pulverized sage, 1 spoon of salt 1 teaspoon of pepper, add 3 dozen oysters, cook altogether 10 minutes. Turn the rice out in a bowl, beat 2 eggs and 1 spoon of butter into it well, add the oysters and gravy, and enough juice from the oysters to make soft. This is enough to dress a medium sized turkey. The oysters can be omited if desired

Mrs Lilly B. Riggs.

Vegetables.

"Oh, better, no doubt is a dinner of herbs
  When seasoned by love, which no rancor disturbs.
And sweetened by all that is sweetest in life.
  Than turbot, bisque. ortolans. eaten in strife."

—Lucile.

Corn Oysters.

6 ears of corn grated, 1 cup cracker crumbs, 2 eggs, 1 tablespoonful sweet cream, pepper and salt to taste. Fry in butter.

MRS ALMA S. WYNN.

Baked Rice.

Take boiled rice, place a layer in a baking dish, then on that a layer of stewed tomatoes, sprinkle with fried minced onions, and repeat the layers till dish is full. Sprinkle over the top with bread crumbs, dot with bits of butter, bake half an hour covered, then uncover and brown.

MRS. J. H. MAGRUDER.

Fried Egg Plant.

Peel and cut the plant in slices less than one half inch thick, immerse in salt water over an hour; drain and dip each slice in beaten egg and bread crumbs, and fry brown.

MISS V. THIBODEAUX.

Stuffed Tomatoes.

Take 4 large tomatoes cut top off and use the inside, chopped fine with parsley, onions, salt and pepper. Mix with this, 1 teaspoonful of butter, 3 tablespoonsful of corn, 3 tablespoonsful of bread crumbs. Then replace in tomato skins and bake.

Mrs. Frank A. Daniels.

Tomato Aspic.

For twelve people 1 can of tomatoes will be required. Steam and put them in a sauce pan with one slice of onion, two bay leaves, a few celery tops, a teaspoonful of salt and a dash of cayenne. Bring to boiling point and add three-quarters of a box of gelatine which has been soaked in one-half cup of cold water for one half hour. Mix until dissolved, add the juice of half a lemon and strain again. Pour into egg cups or moulds and let stand aside on ice for four or five hours. When ready to use plunge the cups in hot water for a minute and turn the aspic out on lettuce leaves. Serve with mayonnaise.

Mrs. F. A. Dicks.

Stuffed Tomatoes,

Take 4 or 5 large tomatoes, slice the top off, then cut out the heart of the tomato, without breaking the skin. Chop the heart with six sweet peppers, a little soaked bread, a teaspoon of butter, salt to taste. Put this back into the tomato skin, sprinkle a little bread crumbs with a little butter on top of each tomato. Bake in a moderate oven till brown.

Miss L. Dirker.

Baked Tomatoes.

Take 6 large ripe tomatoes, skin and cut into small pieces, spread a layer in the bottom of a baking dish, season well, put a layer of coarse bread crumbs over the tomatoes with plenty of butter; continue this until the dish is full, having the bread crumbs on the top. Bake one hour.

How to Fry Plantans.

Slice them and fry. As you take them out of the skillet sprinkle sugar over them. After all are fried, put a tablespoonful of butter in skillet and put all in it. Pour a little warm water over them and sprinkle about a teaspoonful of cinnamon, then set in oven and bake.

ANOTHER.

Slice and fry them till soft, make a thick syrup and pour over them.   Mrs. J. W. Billington.

Green Fried Tomatoes.

Take full grown tomatoes, wash, cut off part next to the stem, cut in thin slices, salt and pepper, fry in hot fat lard and butter mixed. After rolling the slices in flour or meal, fry until brown on both sides.

Mrs. N. L. Jenkins.

Irish Potato Cakes.

Take cold Irish potatoes or fresh boiled ones, mash and add gradually hot water. Make a batter with flour, a teaspoon of Dixie baking powder, pepper and salt. Fry in boiling lard as you do fritters.   Mrs. A. F. G.

Scolloped Onions, Cauliflower or Asparagus.

Boil either vegetable until tender, then put in baking dish and pour over a sauce made of 1 tablespoon butter beat into 1½ tablespoonful of flour; pour over it 1 pint of hot milk and cook until like custard. Bake one half hour, cut cauliflower or asparagus into small pieces before pouring the sauce over it.

Baked Macaroni.

Boil a ½ pound of macaroni in boiling water (salted) till tender, drain and put in a buttered pudding dish in layers with grated cheese between. When your dish is full pour over all this a white sauce and cover well with grated cheese and a little butter, then bake till brown.

White Sauce.

Take ½ pint of milk or milk and water, 1 teaspoon of butter, 1 heaping tablespoon of flour and ¼ teaspoon of salt and pepper. Heat the milk, put the butter into a small sauce pan, stir till it melts and bubbles. Be careful not to brown it. Add the dry flour to the butter, stir quickly till well mixed. Pour ⅓ of the milk, let boil up, stir well as it thickens, then add gradually the rest of milk, and the pepper and salt. Mrs. A. F. G.

Sweet Potato Pone.

1 quart grated sweet potatoes, 2 cups sugar, 1 cup flour 3 eggs, 2 pints milk, 1 small teaspoon of soda, 1 teaspoon alspice. Beat sugar and eggs together, mix with the potatoes and flour, add the milk, soda and spice and bake in a slow oven. Mrs. C. A. Longnecker.

Egg Plant.

Take one egg plant and boil till soft, peel. Put 4 or 5 slices of bread in water; when sufficiently soft squeeze dry and season with a little thyme, onions, pepper and salt. Fry the onion soft. Mix all together, make into cakes and fry brown.

Miss R. Caywood,

RICE.

Take one cup of rice, and two cups of water; let come to a boil, stir once, and put aside where it will cook slowly until all water has evaporated. When dry on top, take off the cover and put another lid under it while it cooks slowly.

Miss R. Caywood.

SPAGHETTI.

Boil very tender 1 pound spaghetti, drain off water and add ¼ pound creamery cheese chopped fine, a large tablespoonful of butter, an onion and two large tomatoes, chopped fine, red pepper and salt to taste. Pour into baking pan and bake slowly until onions are throughly done and spaghetti is brown. A very small piece of garlic adds a flavor.

Mrs. A. Johnson.

Stuffed Potatoes.

Scrape 8 large Irish potatoes; bake and when soft take out center. Have tomatoes and green peas stewed together with a little butter; season highly. Mix with the potatoes taken from the center, fill the shells and return to the oven for ten minutes.

Mrs. Annie Flake.

Macaroni, Italian Style.

Gravy for three pounds of macaroni. Take two or three pounds of meat, beef or pork, brown thoroughly and then take it out of the pot, chop 3 or 4 onions very fine, and brown them thoroughly; add one large size can of tomatoes and brown. Put in the meat let it cook slow for two hours, salt and pepper to suit the taste.

MARY JANE.

Stuffed Cabbage.

Choose a large firm cabbage, take off the outer leaves, and lay cabbage in boiling water 10 minutes, then in cold. Do this several hours before you are ready to stuff it. When cold bind a broad tape about it, that it may not fall apart when the stalk is taken out. Remove the stalk with a sharp knife, leaving a hole as deep as your middle finger. Without widening the mouth, remove the center until you have room for 4 or 5 tablespoonsful of the force meat. Chop the bits you take out very small, mix with some cold boiled pork, ham or cooked sausage meat, a little onion, pepper, salt, pinch of thyme and some bread crumbs. Fill the cavity with this. Bind a wide strip of muslin over the hole in the top and lay cabbage in large sauce pan, with a pint of liquor from boiled ham or beef. Stew gently till tender, take out, unbind carefully, lay on a dish. Add to the strained gravy a piece of butter rolled in flour, 2 tablespoons rich milk, pepper; boil up and pour over the cabbage.

MRS. M. WALKER.

Dread of the dental chair has spoiled many a good meal, we use painless methods in every department.

BOSTON DENTAL CO.,
St. Charles avenue corner Washington

String Beans.

Take off the strings and break them into pieces, cook tender in boiling water, add a little salt, drain them, and put in a hot dish. Butter freely and serve.

MRS. BRIGGS.

SALADS.

Oyster Salad.

Boil two dozen oysters in their own liquor five minutes, drain, wash in cold water, then dry and stand away until very cold. When cold mix with half a cup of Mayonnaise, and serve on crisp lettuce leaves.

Mayonnaise Dressing.

Yolks of two eggs well beaten, half teaspoon of mustard, 1½ teaspoons of vinegar, half teaspoon salt, small half cup of olive oil, pinch of red pepper. Have all the materials as cold as possible. Beat the eggs and mustard one minute and begin adding the oil a drop at a time, beating continually. When like a jelly add a little lemon juice, and begin with a few drops of vinegar at a time, beating all the while. If there is a tendency to curdle, put back on the ice a few minutes. When the vinegar is used up add the salt and pepper, whip five minutes more; pour into a glass and keep on ice until served. Mrs. S. H. Montgomery.

Mock Chicken Salad.

3 lbs. white veal boiled until tender. 8 hard boiled eggs chopped not too fine, 10 cucumber pickles chopped, 3 heads celery chopped, ½ small bottle sweet oil, salt, pepper and vinegar to taste. Mrs. G. P. Work.

Salad Dressing Without Oil.

1 egg, 3 tablespoons vinegar, 1 tablespoon butter, 1 teaspoon mustard, a pinch of salt, a pinch of pepper, put into a pan and stand over boiling water, stirring constantly till quite thick.   Mrs. A. F. Godat.

Chicken Salad.

Boil until thoroughly tender. Then mince the meat very fine, perfectly free from bones and skin. Boil hard 1 dozen eggs. Take the yolks and rub up with vinegar. To this add 1 tablespoon of strong mustard, ½ of black pepper same quantity of salt, 1 cup of melted butter, and one of vinegar. Then mince fine two large stalks of celery, and add all together.   Mrs. S. Henderson.

Fish Salad.

Boil 1 medium red snapper, seasoning well. Have salad dish garnished with lettuce leaves, place fish on it, and dress with a Mayonnaise made as follows: Yolks of 2 raw eggs, yolk of 1 cooked egg, season with a pinch of mustard, cayenne pepper and salt to taste; one pint of sweet oil and juice of 1 lemon.
                     Mrs. E. V. Unsworth.

Cold or Hot Slaw.

1 egg, beat light, 1 tablespoon of dry mustard beat up well with the egg. 2 tablespoons of sugar, salt to taste. ½ head medium sized white cabbage chopped very fine, enough vinegar to moisten the cabbage Mix cabbage and vinegar with all the above ingredients, place on fire and boil up once. Serve hot or cold.
                    Mrs. Alice M. Zable.

Salad Dressing.

One cup vinegar, 2 eggs, 1 tablespoon of butter, 1 teaspoon mustard, 1 teaspoon of sugar, pinch of salt. Boil the vinegar, mix butter, mustard, sugar and salt, beat eggs very light, put together, then pour the boiling vinegar slowly stirring all the time. Return to pan, let cook to boiling point, still stirring. Cool before using. This is excellent for all kinds of salads.

Mrs. A. J. Crebbin.

Salmon Salad.

Take a one pound tin can of the best salmon obtainable, remove it from the can and divide it into not too fine pieces. Line a bowl or platter with lettuce leaves, add the salmon. Squeeze over it a little lemon juice. Mash with dressing, garnish with lemon slices, egg rings, or lettuce.

Lobster Salad.

Use one-third Lobsters, one-third Cod or Halibut and one-third potatoes with water cress or other salad green, use a few spoonfuls of dressing in mixing ingredients, then mask with dressing and decorate.

Mrs. J. W. Billington.

Salad Dressing.

1 tablespoon butter, 1 tablespoon dry mustard, mix to a cream, 2 well beaten eggs, stir in slowly, pepper and salt to taste, add 8 teaspoons of cider vinegar, stirring all the time and cook in a double boiler.

G. F. Cocker.

Tomato Egg Salad.

Place in salad dish a bit of lettuce leaves, then on this
a layer of sliced tomatoes, then a layer of sliced hard boiled eggs, sprinkle over this celery, salt and pepper, and then
another layer of tomatoes and so on till dish is full, over
this pour a mayonnaise dressing. This is a very nice salad.

MRS. E. P. LOWE.

Salmon Salad.

1 can salmon, ½ pound crackers rolled, 3 hard boiled
eggs, 8 small pickles chopped fine, 1 head celery. Salad
dressing: 6 tablespoonfuls vinegar, heated. Take yolks of 2
eggs (raw) and mix into it, 2 tablespoonfuls flour, and butter size of two hickory nuts, salt, pepper, mustard and
sugar. Add this to the scalding vinegar and cook till thick
as cream.

MRS. ALMA S. WYNN.

Chicken Salad.

Take 1 large hen or rooster, boil till quite tender, put
by to cool. Save the jelly oil from water in which chicken
is boiled to add to salad. Boil from 12 to 18 eggs hard.
Then chop up fine 8 or 10 bunches of celery, 1 small bottle of pickles, about 1 tablespoon of mustard, vinegar, salt,
and red and black pepper to taste. Chop up the chicken
and eggs. Mix all well together.

MRS. S. S. KEENER.

EGGS.

Egg Crumb Pie.

6 hard boiled eggs, two cups fine bread crumbs. Put first a layer of bread crumbs in dish, then the thin sliced eggs, little pepper, salt and butter, then another layer of bread crumbs and so on till the dish is filled, last layer to be of eggs; pour over all a cup of sweet milk, and brown in the oven.

Mrs. F. E. McLemore, Delhi, La.

Tom Thumb Omelet.

8 eggs beat well, 1 cup grated cheese, ½ cup sweet milk fry in hot butter, season with salt.

Mrs. J. H. Magruder.

Baked Eggs.

Grease a plate with butter, break the eggs and put on the plate, sprinkle salt and pepper, and a little butter over them and bake in hot oven for a minute or two. This is more digestible than fried eggs.

M. M. W.

Puddings and Sauces

"The proof of the pudding is in the eating"

Royal Diplomatic Pudding.

To 1 box gelatine add 1 glass of water. When dissolved divide into half. To one half add three glasses of granulated sugar, 1 half glass of lemon juice and 1 glass of water. Heat a little to get the sugar to melt, then colour with leaf green. To the other half of gelatine add 2 glasses of sugar and 1 glass of orange juice. Color with red fruit coloring, and when ready to congeal add the whites of 3 eggs beaten to a stiff froth and add to the green. This makes a lovely dessert, looks like water-melon.

Mrs. F. A. Lyons.

Apricot Pudding.

Soak ½ pint of granulated tapioca over night in enough water to cover it. In the morning drain the juice from a can of apricots, stir it into the tapioca, add a half cup of sugar and enough water to make it rather thin. Let this boil until clear. Cover the bottom of a pudding dish with the fruit, sprinkle with sugar, and pour on the tapioca. Bake for half an hour and serve cold with cream.

Mrs. F. A. Dicks.

Jeff. Davis Pudding.

1 tea cup of New Orleans molasses, 1 tea cup of beef suet, 1 tea cup of butter milk, 1 tea cup of raisins (seeded) 1 tea cup of currants, 5 cts. worth of citron cut in pieces as for cakes, 1 teaspoon soda dissolved in butter milk or sifted in the flour, three tea cups of flour after it is sifted; mix molasses and suet first, then alternately butter-milk and flour, then mix the fruit together and flour well, and stir in with a grated nutmeg. Grease a mould well and steam 4 hours. Use boiled sauce as follows: 1 pint granulated sugar, 1 heaping tablespoon of butter, with nutmeg or any other flavoring to taste. J. W. W.

Simple Plum Pudding.

1 cup of molasses, 1 cup of sweet milk, 1 cup of chopped raisins, 1 cup of chopped currants, ½ cup of butter, 3½ cups of flour, 1 teaspoon of soda, 1 teaspoon each of the spices. Dissolve the soda in a little of the syrup, mix all together and put in a double bag and place in boiling water, keep on a steady boil for 3 hours. Keep the pot full of water and the pudding well covered.

Chocolate Pudding.

1 pint milk, 1 pint bread crumbs, ½ cup sugar, 3 eggs, 5 tablespoons grated chocolate. Scald the milk, add bread crumbs and chocolate. Take from fire and add sugar, and the beaten yolks of eggs. Put in pudding dish, bake 15 minutes. Beat the whites of eggs with 1 tablespoon of sugar, spread on and brown. Serve cold with liquid sauce.

Mrs. A. F. G

Fig Pudding.

3 cups bread crumbs, 1 cup milk, 1 cup sugar (brown or white) 1 pound of figs, 1 teaspoon soda, 1 cup suet chopped fine, 2 eggs, spices to taste. Steam 2 hours and serve with hot sauce.

MRS. ALMA S. WYNN.

Portguese Apple Pudding.

Peel, core, and stew to a pulp ½ dozen tart apples; press through a colander; add the grated rind of ½ of a lemon and sufficient sugar to sweeten. Pare, quarter and core 6 more apples, put them in a baking dish, sprinkle ½ cup of sugar over them and bake slowly until tender. Line a deep pie plate with good paste and bake until well colored. Pour into it the stewed apples, piling them up dome shape. Cover with a meringue made of the whites of eggs and a little sugar, eggs beaten to a stiff froth. Brown in a moderate oven and serve cold with a Custard Sauce—yolks of 3 eggs, 1 pint of milk, and 2 tablespoons of sugar.

MRS. ROSENBAUM.

Transparent Pudding.

4 eggs beaten separately, 1 cup butter, 2 cups sugar, beaten together to a cream, add the yolks. Put a layer of citron or acid jelly on the crust, pour on the transperancy, flavor to suit the taste, and bake. then add the whites as a meringue.

AMELIA SCOTT.

Cocoanut Pudding.

Grate 1 cocoanut, 3 slices of bread soaked in the cocoanut milk, 6 eggs beat well with one cup of sugar, 1 pound of raisins, ½ teaspoon Dixie yeast powder.

SAUCE.

½ cup of sugar, ¼ cup of butter well beaten with little cream and nutmeg.

S. H. ANDREWS.

Banana Pudding.

1 box gelatine, 5 bananas, 1 quart milk, 1 pint cream, 2 cups sugar, 1 cup water. Dissolve gelatine in the water, scald milk, to which the sugar has been added. Strain the gelatine, and stir into the milk. Let simmer 10 minutes, cool, slice bananas after peeling into small pieces, and stir into jelly before it is stiff. Serve with whipped cream.

J. W. W.

Rice Pudding.

1 cup of cold rice, yolks of 3 eggs beaten, ½ cup raisins, enough sugar to sweeten, 2 cups sweet milk, beat all together, add a little butter. When baked spread over to top the whites of eggs beaten with sugar, Flavor with Dixie vanilla extract.

M. M. W.

Apple Pudding.

Fill a buttered baking dish, with sliced apples and pour over this a batter made of 1 tablespoon of butter, ½ cup of sugar, 1 egg, ½ cup of sweet milk and 1 cup of flour, 1 teaspoon Dixie yeast powder. Bake in a moderate oven till brown. Serve with cream and sugar or liquid sauce.

Boiled Pudding.

1 cup suet chopped fine, 1 cup of raisins cut in half, 2 cups flour, 1 cup milk, 1 cup sugar, a little nutmeg and a little salt, 1 teaspoon Dixie yeast powder. Grease and flour a tin bucket, put pudding in and boil hard for 2 hours. Serve with a rich sauce. MISS M. KEEN.

Lemon Pudding.

1½ pound of sugar, juice and grated rind of 3 lemons, 8 eggs, 1 cup of butter, tablespoon of flour. Beat well together, and bake. MRS. OLIVER.

Pies and Pastry.

"No soil upon earth is so dear to our eyes,
As the soil we first stirred in terrestrial pies.
—*O. H. Holmes.*

Mock Mince Pies.

1 cup bread crumbs dried, and 2 cups seeded and
chopped (rolled) raisins, ½ cup molasses, 1 lemon, juice
and grated rind, nutmeg, cinnamon, and whatever spice is
desired. Sugar to taste, little water.

Mrs. F. R. H.

Cream Pie.

Beat thoroughly the yolks of 2 eggs with ½ cup of
sugar, add 1 heaping tablespoon of flour, 1 even tablespoon
of corn starch dissolved in milk. Pour into 1 pint of boiling
milk and let cook about 3 minutes. Let cool and flavor to
taste.

M. B.

Pastry for Pies.

Sieve 3 cups flour in a pan, salt to taste, add 1 cup
lard, mix thoroughly with half the flour. Add ½ cup water,
mould lightly; roll out, and put it in pans, pricking it over
with a knife to prevent blistering.

Lemon Pie.

1 quart of sweet milk, (condensed milk will do as well) the yolks of 5 eggs, 2 heaping tablespoons of corn starch, about 2 cups of sugar or sweeten to taste, 2 lemons the grated rind and juice, put the milk on to boil, beat the yolk of eggs, sugar and lemons together, mix the corn-starch with a little milk, put into the boiling milk, and when it thickens add the eggs, lemon and sugar. Let all cook till it has thickened enough, then stir in a teaspoon of butter, and when cold add Dixie Vanilla Flavoring. Have the pie crust already cooked, put the mixture in and put in the oven to cook a few minutes, then spread over the pies the whites of the eggs which have been beaten up with 4 spoons of sugar, brown a little in the oven.

Mrs. J. W. Wilkinson.

Filling for Lemon Pies.

Grate the yellow covering and squeeze out the juice of 2 lemons into a granite pan; add 2 cups flour, 2 cups sugar, the yolks of 4 eggs, reserving the whites in a separate dish, add 4 tablespoonsful flour, 2 cups water added slowly while stirring. When smooth, cook until thick enough to pour into the crust, which should be already baked. Beat the 4 whites of eggs into a froth, add 1 cup sugar, 1 tea-spoonful of Dixie lemon extract. Pour over the pies, return to oven until the white top becomes a light brown.

Mrs. N. L. Jenkins.

Lemon Pie.

1 large lemon, 1 cup sugar, ½ cup of water, 2 eggs, 1 teaspoon of flour. Grate lemon, using it in the juice, mix juice and eggs together, then stir in sugar, mixing well, mix the water, then flour lastly.

PASTE.

1 cup flour, (with a pinch of salt) sifted, rub in 2 tablespoons of lard, then roll out for pie pan.

MRS. FRANK A. DANIELS.

Orange Pie.

Slice 3 oranges, peel, take out the pits. Leave them over-night in sugar, next day put the sliced oranges on a well made pie crust in a pie pan. Then take the yolks of 8 eggs, 1½ cups of powdered sugar, lemon juice and grated rind of 1 lemon. Put it on the stove and stir constantly till it thickens. Beat the white of the eggs to a froth, and mix all together. Now pour it on your oranges and bake.

MRS. ADLER.

Transparent Custard.

6 eggs, 2 cups of sugar, 1 cup of butter, 1 tablespoon of cornstarch and Dixie vanilla extract, beat butter and sugar to a cream, then add the yolks beaten to a froth with the cornstarch and extract. Stir all together and bake in nice crust. When done spread the beaten whites of eggs and 6 tablespoons of sugar, over the pie and brown slightly.

MRS. F. E. McLEMORE, Delhi, La.

Custard Fruit Pie.

Make a good pie crust, rub a little flour on it and lay on your pie plates. Put stewed fruit in it and pour over them a custard made with 2 eggs, 1 cup of milk and a cup of sugar, beaten together. Enough for 2 pies.

Mrs. A. F. Godat.

Sweet Potato Pies.

Boil 5 large sweet Pototoes till soft, mash and season with sugar, butter, 2 eggs, nutmeg and a cup of milk, mix all together and put in the crust enough for 3 pies.

Miss Caywood.

Mince Meat.

1 beef tongue, 2 pounds of raisins, 2 pounds of currants, 2 dozen of apples, $\frac{1}{2}$ pound of beef suet, $\frac{1}{2}$ pound of citron, 2 tablespoons of cinnamon, 2 tablespoons of nutmeg, 2 tablespoons of mace, 1 tablespoon of cloves, 1 tablespoon of allspice, 1 tablespoon of salt, $2\frac{1}{2}$ pounds of brown sugar, 1 quart of cider. Use ground spice. Chop all up finely, put in jar and cover up.

Mrs. W. W. Sutcliffe.

CAKES.

Watermelon Cake.

1½ cups sugar, whites of 4 eggs, ½ cup sweet milk, ½ cup of butter, 2 cups of flour, 1 full teaspoon Dixie baking powder. Cream butter and sugar well together, then add the milk, afterward stir in a little flour, then a little egg, and so on until all the ingredients are added. Then take 1½ cups of pink sugar (any good confectioner can supply it) ½ cup sour milk, 2 cups flour, 1 teaspoonful Dixie baking powder. Flavor the pink part with anything you prefer, rose water is much used. Seed ¼ pound of good raisins, rub well in flour, to prevent them sinking. After the dough of both kinds are ready, spread the bottom and sides of the pan with the white dough; fill up with the pink, leaving enough of the white to cover over top entirely. Bake carefully. Be sure it is well done before removing from the pan. This cake is very popular with young people. MRS. FLORENCE E. RUSS.

Sponge Cake.

10 eggs, beat separate; 1 pound of sugar, ½ pound of flour, 1 tablespoonful of Dixie baking powder. Flavor with lemon, add the whites of the eggs last.

MISS MOLLIE WALKER.

Velvet Sponge Cake.

2 eggs, beaten light; beat in 1 cupful of granulated or powdered sugar, ½ cupful of sifted flour, next ½ cupful of flour sifted with 1 teaspoonful of Dixie baking powder, and lastly, ½ cupful of boiling water very gradually. Have the tin buttered. Fill and bake immediately in a well heated oven. The batter will seem very thin, but the cake is excellent. By the use of one more egg any layer cake may be made better than with butter. For this save 2 whites out for frosting, using the other egg and 2 yolks for the cake. Bake in layer cake tins. Whip the whites stiff, and stir in sugar. Spread between each layer, and over the top. For cocoanut cake sprinkle cocoanut over the frosting between the layers, and thickly over the top layer. For chocolate, grate ½ teacupful of Baker's chocolate, and stir in the frosting, and use as before.

Sponge Cake.

Separate the whites and yolks of 4 eggs. When the whites are stiff enough, beat into them ½ cup of sugar, beating for 5 minutes. Add to the yolks the juice and grated rind of a lemon. Now beat well together the yolks and whites. Add 1 cup of flour stirring it in as lightly as possible. (Never beat a sponge cake after adding the flour) Bake for 25 minutes in a moderate oven. Just before putting in the oven sprinkle on the top through a sifter, about a tablespoonful of granulated sugar.

MRS. D. ROSENBAUM.

Molasses Sponge Cake.

1 cup of molasses, 2½ cups of flour, ½ cup of shortening, ½ cup of sugar, a little salt, 1 teaspoon of cinnamon, 1 teaspoon of ginger. Mix and add 1 teaspoon of soda dissolved in a cup of boiling water.

Mrs. P. R. Baldwin, Biloxi, Miss.

Layer Sponge Cake.

1½ cups powdered sugar, 5 eggs, 3 tablespoons water, 2 cups flour, 2 level teaspoons Dixie baking powder.

COOKED ICING FILLING.

1½ cups granulated sugar, 9 tablespoons water, cook until it begins to rope. Pour it into the whites of three eggs, well beaten and beat this until it cools, mix with it pecans or chocolate or any you prefer, and spread between layers of cake. This will make four good layers.

Miss Mary Werlein.

Buffalo Layer Cake.

1 cup of white sugar, two-thirds cup of sweet milk, 2 cups of flour, 1 egg, 1 tablespoon melted butter, 1 teaspoon Dixie baking powder. Bake in 3 jelly tins.

CREAM FILLING.

1 cup sweet milk, 1 egg, 1 tablespoon cornstarch, 2 tablespoons sugar. Heat the milk until boiling with the sugar in it, then add the starch wet in a little cold milk, stir until it thickens, put in lastly the egg well beaten.

Miss Mary Werlein.

Fruit Cake.

One pound each of butter, sugar, flour, raisins, (seeded and chopped) and currants thoroughly cleaned, ½ pound of citron shaved fine, and 1 pound or more of nuts, cut fine. Cream the butter and sugar together, to which add the well beaten yolks of eight eggs, then a part of the flour, then add a part of the whites, beaten to a stiff froth; then the remainder of the flour, (except a little kept out to mix with the fruit, just before putting it in the cake). After adding all the whites, beat well; then put in the fruit, and mix thoroughly. Bake slowly until done.

Fruit Cake.

2 pounds of sugar. 2 pounds of flour, 2 pounds of butter, 2 pounds of dried currants, 2 pounds of raisins, 2 pounds of citron, ½ spoonful of cloves. and ½ of a nutmeg, 12 eggs, whites beaten to a stiff froth.

Mrs. G. V. Pierce, Biloxi, Miss.

Cake and Sauce.

2 cups sugar, 1 cup butter, 1 cup milk, 4 eggs, 3½ cups of flour, 1 teaspoon vanilla extract. 2 teaspoons Dixie baking powder. Beat butter and sugar to a cream, add yolks of eggs, milk and flavoring, add flour reserving two tablespoonfuls; add whites of eggs. Put baking powder in the reserved flour and add to cake.

SAUCE

Whites of 2 eggs, beat light, add 3 tablespoons of powdered sugar, yolks of 2 eggs, and 3 tablespoons of milk 1 teaspoon of vanilla. Prepare immediately before serving.

Miss Fannie M. Rayne.

Cocoanut Pound Cake.

Beat ½ pound of butter to a cream; add gradually a
pound of sifted flour, 1 pound of powdered sugar, 2 teaspoonsful of Dixie baking powder, a pinch of salt, a teaspoonful of grated lemon-peel, ¼ of a pound of prepared
cocoanut, 4 well-beaten eggs, and a cup of milk; mix thoroughly; butter the tins, and line them with buttered paper;
pour the mixture in to the depth of an inch and a half,
and bake in a good oven. When baked, take out, spread
icing over them, and return the cake to the oven a moment
to dry the icing. Perfection cake.

Mrs. Pierce.

Citron Pound Cake.

1 cup butter, 2 cups sugar, 2 cups flour, 4 eggs, 1½ teaspoons Dixie baking powder, 1 teaspoon essence, 5 cts. worth
of citron. Icing; white of 1 egg, 8 tablespoons pulverized
sugar.   Mrs. Rosenbaum.

If the teeth are sensitive to sweets half the pleasure is
lost. This condition should be remedied without delay.

Boston Dental Co.,
St. Charles avenue corner Washington.

Cornstarch Cake.

½ cup butter, creamed; ½ cup of sugar, ½ cup of milk,
½ teaspoon almond extract, ½ cup cornstarch, 1½ cups of
flour, ¼ teaspoon of soda, ½ teaspoon cream of tartar, whites
of 6 eggs. Mix in the order given and bake in a moderate
oven.   Mrs. Holmes.

White Cup Cake.

1 cup butter, 2 cups sugar, 1 cup milk, 3 cups flour. white of 12 eggs, flavoring to suit taste, $\frac{1}{2}$ teaspoon of Dixie baking powder.

Another White Cup Cake.

4 cups flour, 2 cups butter, 1 cup milk, 3 cups sugar, Whites of 20 eggs, 1 small teaspoon Dixie baking powder.

Mrs. F. E. McLemore, Delhi, La.

White Cake.

Whites of 8 eggs, well whipped; 3 cups pulverized sugar, 1 cup butter, 1 cup milk, 4 cups sifted flour with 1 teaspoon cream of tartar, $\frac{1}{2}$ teaspoon soda, dissolved in milk, juice of 1 lemon. Bake 1 hour in a moderate oven.

Mrs. Buchell.

A Nice White Cake.

Beat the whites of 5 eggs, very light; add 1 cup of sugar, $\frac{3}{4}$ cup of butter, 2 cups of flour, 2 small teaspoonfuls of Dixie baking powder. Bake in a small loaf.

Tchoupitoulas Mission.

Sponge Cake.

Sift 1 cup flour, 1 cup sugar and 1 teaspoon Dixie baking powder together, then break 3 eggs into it, and only beat enough to get a smooth batter.

Mrs. Annie Flake.

White Nut Cake.

The whites of 7 eggs, 3 cups flour, 1 teaspoon vanilla, 3 teaspoons Dixie baking powder, 2 cups pulverized sugar, 2 cups milk, ¾ cup butter, cream the butter and sugar; then add the flour and milk alternately; then add the whites well beaten. Bake this in 4 layers, 1½ pounds pecans cut fine (reserving 30 whole to put on the top). Beat the whites of 5 eggs and 1 full cup of pulverized sugar together until very stiff; add the cut pecans for the filling. Ice the top, split the 30 pecans and lay them on the top in the icing. AMELIA SCOTT.

Nut Cake.

2 cups of sugar, two-thirds cup of butter, 4 eggs, two-thirds cup of water or milk, 3 cups of flour, 3 teaspoons Dixie baking powder, 1 cup of nuts. Bake in shallow baking pans, and cut into squares with icing. Currants may be substituted for nuts.

MISS MAY WILLIAMS.

Nut Cake.

1 pound flour, 1 pound sugar, ¼ lb. butter, 6 eggs, 1 cup sweet milk, 1 grated nutmeg, 1¼ pounds raisins stoned, 3 pounds hulled pecans, 1 teaspoon Dixie baking powder. Cream the butter and sugar, beat the eggs very light, all together, and add to butter and sugar, then the milk, flour and baking powder, then the raisins and nuts. Bake in a slow oven until a straw will come out without anything sticking to it. MRS. M. A. RILEY.

Lemon Cake.

4 eggs, 1 cup sugar, 1 cup flour, ½ teaspoon Dixie baking powder, 1 tablespoon cold water, ¼ lemon, juice and rind. Mix the yolks of the eggs and sugar together, then add the water, sift the flour and measure out an even cupful. Stir this thoroughly, then the whites of the eggs beaten to a stiff dry froth, then the lemon juice and grated rind, and lastly the baking powder. Cook in pie or jelly pans.

FILLING

One cup of hot water, 1 tablespoon of cornstach, 1 cup of white sugar, 1 tablespoon of butter, juice and grated rind of one lemon, 1 egg. Cook a few minutes and spread between each cake like jelly.

Miss Mollie Walker.

Marble Cake.

Whites of 7 eggs, 1 cup of butter, 2 cups of sugar, ½ cup sweet milk, then 3½ cups flour, 1 tablespoonful of Dixie baking powder.

DARK PART.

Yolks of 7 eggs, 1 cup of molasses, 2 cups of brown sugar, ½ cup of butter, 1 cup of sweet milk, 5 cups of flour, 1 tablespoonful Dixie baking powder, 1 tablespoonful of different spices except ginger, 1 teaspoonful of ginger is enough. Grease cake pan, then put in a layer of the white batter then the dark and so on, until you have enough in the pan. Bake 1 hour.

Miss Mollie Walker.

Lemon Cream Layer Cake.

1 cup of butter, 2 cups sugar, 3 cups flour and 4 eggs, 2 teaspoons Dixie baking powder.   Bake in 4 layers.

FILLING.

2 eggs, 1 cup of sugar, beat very light.   Boil 2 cups of sweet milk; when the milk comes to a boil stir in 7 spoonfuls of cornstarch wet up in cold milk.   Then stir in the eggs and sugar, let cook a moment, pour out in a dish and flavor with grated rind and juice of 2 lemons, and spread between layers of cake.

Lemon Jelly Filling.

The juice of two lemons, and grated rind of one, one cupful of sugar, one egg, half cupful of water, one tablespoonful of butter, one tablespoonful of flour mixed with a little water.   Cook over boiling water until it thickens.   Place between the layers of cake.   This cake will keep well and is better at the end of a week than it is the first day.

MRS. PIERCE.

Marshmallow Cake.

1 cup of butter, 2 cups of sugar, 3 cups of flour, 2 teaspoons of Dixie baking powder, 1 cup of sweet milk, white of 6 eggs, cream, butter and sugar, add milk and flour, lastly eggs beaten stiff in three layers.

FILLING

2 cups granulated sugar, ½ cup boiling water, let boil. Whites of 2 eggs beaten stiff, put 16 marshmallows in a slow oven to heat.   When the syrup threads when poured from a spoon, pour over the eggs and beat well, add marshmallows, beat smooth and spread.   Excellent.

Caramel Cake.

¾ of a pound of butter, whites of 10 eggs, 3 cups granulated sugar, ¾ cup of water, 1 quart unsifted flour, one teaspoon Dixie baking powder. Bake in jelly cake pans.

CARAMEL FOR FILLING FOR THE ABOVE.

4 cups brown sugar, 1 cup of cream or milk, half cup of butter, vanilla. Put all together and stew until it is about the consistency of molasses, then fill your cakes. A few hulled and well-broken pecans sprinkled over the caramel before putting on next layer adds very much to it. Ornament top with half pecans.

Caramel Cake.

2 eggs, 1 cup of brown sugar, ½ cup of butter, ½ cup of milk, ¼ teaspoonful of soda, 1 teaspoonful of cream of tartar; 2 cups of flour.

FOR FILLING.

2 cups sugar, two-thirds cup of milk, butter nearly as large as an egg. Boil 10 minutes, beat till almost cold, and flavor with vanilla. This is very nice; try it.

MRS. FLORENCE E. RUSS.

Lady Cake.

½ cup butter, 1 cup sugar, 3 cups flour, 1 cup luke warm water, 5 eggs (whites) 2 teaspoons Dixie baking powder, 1 teaspoon of essence. Cream butter, stir in the sugar then ½ of the water, then a tablespoon of the flour, alternating with the water, then one half of the eggs beaten stiff' then your powder, then the rest of eggs.

MRS. ROSENBAUM.

Angel Food Cake Filling.

Grate 1 cocoanut, 1 pound of grated chocolate, take the white of 4 eggs, 1 pound of powdered sugar, let it cook as in boiled icing. When it begins to rope take half of it and mix with the chocolate, the other half mix with cocoanut, reserving enough of the cocoanut to sprinkle on top of the cake. Spread over the first layer of cake the chocolate filling, then the next layer the cocoanut filling, and so on till it is the desired size, the cocoanut filling to be on top of cake. Mrs. Oliver.

Wine Cakes.

1 ounce of Fleshmen's yeast dissolved in ½ pint water; add flour to make thick batter, set it to rise. When it rises sufficiently, add the yolks of 4 eggs, 1 tablespoonful of butter, a little nutmeg, a few drops of Dixie lemon extract, and flour to make a thick batter, set aside for 30 minutes. Grease and flour 12 or 15 small fancy cake moulds, fill them ¾ full; let them rise ½ hour, put in oven and bake 20 or 25 minutes. For the syrup take 1 pound white sugar, 1 cup water ⅓ of a lemon, a piece of nutmeg or mace, a small piece of cinnamon, cook to a string syrup, flavor with unfermented wine. When cakes are baked soak thoroughly in syrup, set in a seive to drain. The Manhattan.

Hickory Nut Cake.

Cake same as for Marshmallow Filling, 1 cup of sour cream, 1 cup of sugar, 1 cup of hickory nut meat, chopped fine, boil all together, cool and spread between the layers.

Delicious Cake.

1 cup of sugar, 2 eggs, ½ cupful of butter, ½ cupful of milk, and 1½ cupfuls of flour, unsifted; cream the butter and sugar together, beat the eggs light, and mix well, then add ½ teaspoonful of Dixie baking powder, and bake in a moderate oven. This makes a delicious layer cake.

Cake Featherweight.

2 tablespoons butter, 6 eggs (reserve 2 whites for icing) 2 cups sugar. 3 cups flour, 2 teaspoons Dixie baking powder, ½ cup milk, ¼ pound chocolate, vanilla extract to taste, 1 teaspoonful cinnamon. Bake in jelly tins with anything between layers.

MISS COCKER.

Lip Kucke (German Fruit Cake).

6 eggs, 1 cup brown sugar, 1 cup black molasses, ½ pound grated chocolate, 1 cup pecans (chopped), ½ pound citron, allspice and cinnamon to suit taste, 3 cups flour, 1 teaspoonful Dixie baking powder. Bake in a moderate oven. Slice and ice. MISS COCKER.

Eggless Cake.

1 cup of sugar, 1 cup of sour milk, 1 cup of chopped raisins, ½ cup of butter, 2 cups of flour, 1 teaspoon of Dixie baking powder, ¼ of a teaspoon of each of the spices; cinnamon, cloves and nutmeg.

MRS. D. ROSENBAUM.

Creams and Custards.

"But please your honor, quoth the Peasant,
This same dessert is very pleasant."

—*Pope.*

Floating Island.

Put one pint of milk into a double boiler. Separate 3 eggs, beat the whites to a stiff froth, drop them by spoonfuls over the top of the milk, allow them to remain for just a moment, then lift carefully. Beat the yolks of the eggs with two tablespoons of sugar; add them to the hot milk, cook till the mixture slightly thickens. Be very careful that it does not curdle; take from the fire, add a teaspoon of vanilla and turn into the dish in which it is to be served. Heap the whites of the eggs over the top and serve cold.

Mrs. Peirce.

Orange or Pineapple Ambrosia.

Have the orange or pineapple broken up into tiny pieces. Beat to a stiff froth the whites of 2 eggs with sugar. Place in a glass bowl a layer of the fruit, sprinkle over it a little sugar, then spread on a little of the beaten egg, over that sprinkle grated cocoanut, then another layer of fruit, and so on till the dish is full.

Mrs. Minnie Wilkinson.

Pineapple Sponge.

1 small fresh pineapple, or a can of the fruit. Must be chopped up and put with its juice in a sauce pan with a small cupful of sugar and a cupful of water. If canned pineapple is used add less sugar. Simmer 10 minutes, ½ a package of gelatine should be soaked in ½ a cupful of water for two hours. When ready add the gelatine, take from the fire at once, and strain into a tin basin. Set the basin in a pan of ice water or in the refrigerator, and when the mixture begins to thicken, stir in the whites of 4 eggs, beaten to a stiff froth. Pour into a mould and set away to harden. Serve with cream.

MRS. F. A. DICKS.

PEACH FLOAT.

· 1 pint canned peaches, cook ten minutes, the whites of three eggs well beaten, add a tablespoonful at a time until thoroughly mixed, then beat in sugar to taste. A very nice dessert.   MRS. F. A. LYONS.

Charlotte Russe.

1 quart of thick cream, ½ pint of milk, 1 ounce of gelatine, yolks of 5 eggs, whites of 7 eggs, 12 ounces of sugar. Dissolve the gelatine in the boiling milk; take it off the fire and stir in the yolks of eggs, then the sugar and Dixie vanilla flavoring. When the custard is cool, before it congeals, stir in the cream, whipped to a froth, and then the beaten whites of the eggs.

Tapioca Cream.

Take two tablespoons of tapioca soaked over night, or say three hours, in water enough to cover it. Boil this with one quart of new milk in a double boiler. Add one cup of sugar and a little salt. Beat the yolks of 3 eggs thoroughly, and stir them into the milk when it has boiled ten minutes. Remove from the fire and stir rapidly for 5 minutes. Flavor with one teaspoonful of Dixie Vanilla, pour into a baking dish, beat the whites of the eggs to a stiff froth, pour over the top. Sift sugar over this and brown. Serve cold with cream.

Mrs. F. A. Dicks.

Cocoanut Charlotte Russe.

Make a sponge cake in a deep round pan, cut out the centre leaving about an inch of crust. Fill with cocoanut custard, cover the top with whipped cream, put in a cold place till needed.

Cocoanut Custard.

6 eggs, white of 5, 1 pint of milk, 1 cup sugar, 1 cup cocoanut. 1 teaspoon corn starch, 1 teaspoon Dixie Vanilla flavoring, small cup of cream whipped light with the white of 1 egg.

Mrs. Annie Flake.

Ambrosia.

Place in a glass bowl alternate layers of sliced oranges and grated cocoanut, sprinkling sugar on each layer of orange. Having top layer cocoanut.

Mrs. Oliver.

Strawberry Float.

1 pint of strawberries, 2 eggs, 2 cups of pulverized sugar, 1 pint of milk, vanilla flavoring. Crush the berries. Separate the whites of the eggs from the yolks, beat the former to a stiff dry froth, and add the sugar. Put in crushed berries gradually, beating all the while until the whole is a stiff pile of rosy cream, place in glass dish and set on ice. Beat the yolks of the eggs in half a cupful of the milk, place remainder of milk on the stove in pan set in another containing boiling water. When the milk is hot add sugar, eggs and vanilla to taste, and set on ice to cool. This sauce is to be poured in serving about the frothy berries.

Mrs. J. W. Wilkinson.

Lemon Cream.

Yolks of 4 eggs, 4 tablespoons granulated sugar, juice and grated rind of 1 lemon, 2 tablespoons boiling water. Let simmer till it thickens. When cold, just before serving, add the whites beaten with 2 tablespoons of sugar, mixing thoroughly.

Miss May Williams.

Sherbet and Ice Cream.

Freeze ice cream in a warm place, the cream freezes more rapidly when the ice melts quick.

Vanilla Ice Cream.

Put one quart of milk on to boil in double boiler. Beat together the yolks of 6 eggs, 6 tablespoons of sugar, stir into boiling milk, cook about a minute, stirring constantly. Strain it, allow to cool, add 1 tablespoon of Dixie Vanilla and the beaten whites of eggs and freeze.

MRS. BRIGGS.

Lemon Ice Cream.

6 lemons, 3 quarts milk, 1½ pints sugar. Pour milk over the lemon peels and let it stand 1 hour, strain and sweeten, and when nearly frozen, stir in the juice of the lemons. This makes one gallon.

MISS MARY WERLEIN.

Bravarian Ice Cream.

Sweeten 1 pint of cream to taste, flavor with vanilla or lemon. Churn the cream to a froth; skim the froth as it rises, and put in a glass dish. Dissolve 1½ tablespoons of gelatine in warm water, pour into the froth and stir for 15 minutes. Pack or set in ice, and it will be ready for use in a few hours.   MRS. S. S. KEENER.

Caramel Ice Cream.

Melt 1½ pounds of brown sugar in the frying pan until liquid, stirring all the time. Do not let it scorch or get too dark. Pour the caramel into a pint of boiling milk by degrees, mixing well. When cold strain into three quarts of cream or milk and freeze. 1 pint of the cream may be whipped and added as directed. MRS. D. ROSENBAUM.

Lemon Sherbet.

Two-thirds can of condensed milk, 3 lemons, juice and grated rind, sugar to taste. White of 2 eggs, beat and put in when nearly frozen. This is for ½ gallon, add water enough to nearly fill the can. MRS. F. R. H.

Philadelphia Ice Cream.

2 cans condensed milk, 4 cans cows milk, 2 cans sweet cream; whites of 2 eggs, whipped to a stiff froth. Flavor to taste with vanilla or lemon; add whites just before freezing.

Mrs. S. S. Keener.

Peach Ice Cream.

1 pint cream, 1 pint milk, 1 cup sugar, 1 quart peach pulp. Rub the peaches through a sieve to produce a pulp, add a small quantity of the sugar and set aside. Place the cream and milk over the fire to allow them to come exactly to the boiling point, remove and stir in the remainder of the sugar and set aside to cool, then add the peach pulp and freeze.

Mrs. G. M. Quarles.

Cream Cheese Ice Cream.

5 cream cheese, sweeten and flavor to taste; add 1 quart of sweet milk and freeze.

Mrs. Annie Flake.

Strawberry Cream Cheese Ice Cream.

3 cream cheese, separate the cream from the cheese, mash cheese to a paste, add one can of condensed milk, and sugar to taste, add the cream; then 1½ pint of sweet milk, 1 glass ice cold water, Dixie Vanilla Flavoring, the beaten whites of 2 eggs, and lastly the mashed and sweetened strawberries. Beat all together well and freeze. This makes ¾ gal. delicious cream.

Mrs. E. P. Lowe.

Chocolate Cream.

12 eggs, 3 cups sugar, ½ gallon milk, ½ cup chocolate or cocoa, vanilla extract. Beat all the eggs, except the whites of 3 with the sugar and chocolate; add the milk and then boil to a thin custard. When it it begins to freeze, add the whites of the eggs.

Mrs. Annie Flake.

Coffee Frozen.

· Prepare the coffee as for the table; add cream and sugar, making it sweeter than for drinking. Freeze and serve in after dinner coffee cups. Mrs. Oliver.

Pineapple Snow.

1 gallon rich milk, 1 can pineapple, 1 pound of sugar; beat all together and freeze.

Mrs. H. W. Knickerbocker.

Frozen Cream Cheese.

One quart of sweet milk to 6 cream cheeses, with the cream, ½ teaspoon of soda. Sweeten to taste, flavor with Dixie Vanilla Extract. Mrs. Holmes.

Bisque.

½ gallon cream whipped, yolks of 9 eggs, 3 pounds of granulated sugar. Mix the eggs with ½ gallon of milk which has been boiled with vanilla bean in it, add the sugar to the whipped cream, then mix all ingredients together, beating well. Then freeze. This makes about 24 bisques. Miss Wasson.

⊰⊰⊰⊰*Candies.*⊱⊱⊱⊱

Pecan Candy.

Take two large cups of granulated sugar, put into a dry pot and stir constantly till every bit of sugar is dissolved. Soon as it becomes a syrup pour it over your prepared nuts. In a few minutes it will be cold enough to cut into small pieces. P. S. M.

Pecan Candy.

1 cup sugar, white of one egg, 1 cup pecans, (picked well) stir and mix well without beating, place thin layer in pie pan, bake light brown in moderately hot oven.
MRS. J. H. MAGRUDER.

Caramel Candy.

One cake Baker's chocolate (not sweet, ½ lb.) 3 pounds brown sugar, ¼ pound butter. 1 tea cup milk. Mix milk and sugar and boil well together, then add the butter, stiring until melted, then add the grated chocolate and boil hard until done. Test by dropping on a plate and cooling rapidly. MRS. CHRISTIAN KEENER.

Cocoanut Pralines.

One cup of peeled and grated cocoanut, two cups of sugar ½ cup of water. Put sugar and water on to boil, cook it until when dropped in cold water it is brittle, add a piece of butter size of a walnut, put in the grated cocoanut, and cook just a few minutes, then drop on buttered plates or tins. For the white use white sugar, for the brown pralines, the best brown sugar, and to color them pink, use fruit coloring. MISS CLARA BILLINGTON

Pickles and Preserves.

In making pickles the vinegar should be very strong and should only be brought to the boiling point and immediately poured on pickles. Cook in porcelain or granite kettle. Never put up pickles in anything that has held grease of any kind. The nicest way to put up pickles is bottling; sealing while hot and keeping in a cool dark place. The brine for pickles should be strong enough to bear an egg; make it in the proportion of a heaping pint of coarse salt to a gallon of water.

Sweet Pickles.

$\frac{1}{2}$ peck green tomatoes, sliced; 9 cucumbers, 1 head cabbage, 1 dozen seed onions, 3 pods of green pepper. Place in a jar alternately with salt and let stand over night. 1 ounce each of white and black mustard seed, $\frac{1}{2}$ ounce turmeric, 1 ounce celery seed, $\frac{1}{2}$ box mustard, 1 pound sugar. Mix together with cider vinegar. Let it come to a boil, then put in a jar and seal.

Mrs. W. W. Sutcliffe.

Sweet Pickle Peaches.

1 quart good vinegar, 2 cups of sugar, 1 teaspoon of cinnamon. Stick 2 or 3 whole cloves in peaches. After peeling, put fruit in with sugar and vinegar; boil till fruit is very tender, and juice thickened.

Mrs. Ella Everett, Shubuta, Miss.

Chow-Chow.

1 peck tomatoes, 5 onions, 3 heads cabbage, 1 dozen green peppers. Chop all separately, then mix well, put in salt and let drain all night. Put in a kettle one pound of brown sugar, ½ teaspoon grated horseradish, 1 teaspoon ground black pepper, 1 teaspoon ground mustard, 1 tablespoon of celery seed and 1 tablespoon of white mustard seed. Cover with a pint of vinegar, boil and pour over chopped mixture.   MRS. W. W. SUTCLIFFE.

Chow-Chow.

1 dozen onions, 1 peck green tomatoes. 4 heads of cabbage, 1 dozen cucumbers, (in brine 3 days), 3 oz. white mustard seed, 1 oz. celery seed, 4 tablespoons whole pepper, 1 oz. turmeric, small box of mustard, 2½ lbs. brown sugar. Chop onions, cabbage and tomatoes day before and sprinkle with salt in proportion, ½ pt. to a peck; next day drain out brine. Tablespoon pulverized alum. Put all in kettle cover with weak vinegar, 3 tablespoons of turmeric let it come to a boil then drain off. Then cover with strong vinegar and add all the spice and sugar, simmer slowly ½ hour and bottle.   MRS. F. A. LYONS.

Spiced Grapes.

Small dark grapes are excellent for this. 5 pounds grapes, 4 pounds sugar, 1 quart vinegar, 1 tablespoon cinnamon, 1 tablespoon cloves. Cook for sometime, skimming off the seeds as they rise to top, in cooking. Cook down to a sauce. To eat with vegetables.
                   MRS. ELLA EVERETT, Shubuta, Miss.

Green Tomato Sweet Pickles.

Slice 1 gallon green tomatoes and salt well. Let stand until morning, drain and pour on fresh water, let stand 2 or 3 hours. Slice 12 large onions; put in kettle a layer of tomatoes and a layer of onions, cover with best vinegar and boil until tender; then add 1 tablespoon of mace, 1 tablespoon of spice, 1 tablespoon of nutmeg, 1 tablespoon black pepper, 1 tablespoon mustard, 1 tablespoon cloves, 1 pound brown sugar 1 oz. white mustard seed.

Mrs. S. S. KEENER.

Green Tomato Sauce, or Soy.

2 gallons green tomatoes without peeling, sliced; 12 large onions, 2 quarts best vinegar, 1 quart sugar, 2 tablespoons salt, 2 tablespoons ground mustard, 1 tablespoon black pepper, 1 tablespoon allspice, 1 tablespoon cinnamon, ground; 1 tablespoon cloves. Mix all together, stew until tender, stir often to prevent scorching; put in fruit jars. A fine soy for all kinds of fish and meat.

Mrs. ELLA EVERETT.

Peach Sweet Pickles.

Make a syrup of 1 quart of vinegar, 5 pounds of sugar, 1 tablespoonful each of cloves, allspice and stick cinnamon. Tie the spice in a thin cloth, drop into the syrup, let come to a good boil. If the fruit is peaches, peel them and leave stones in; if pears, peel and core. Take 8 pounds of the fruit and add to syrup (after the fruit has been through the lime water preparation). Let the fruit boil until it is transparent and begins to sink in the syrup, when it is ready for the jars. Mrs. J. B. WALKER,
Mississippi City.

Preparation for Preserving Ripe Fruit.

Have 1 gallon of cold water in an earthern bowl. Put in the water 1 large teacup of unslacked lime, stir well, then put in as much fruit as water will cover. Let stand about 6 minutes, then rinse in clear water (do not let it remain in the water); continue putting your fruit in lime water and then in clear, until the kettleful is prepared. Let the fruit remain in lime water two minutes longer, every bowl full as the acid weakens the lime. This lime water will prepare a large kettle of fruit. The lime water toughens the fruit so it can be boiled, also assists in preventing the preserves from fermenting.

Mrs. J. B. Walker.

Spiced Currants.

Wash thoroughly 1 pound of currants. Cover with cold water and vinegar equal parts, 1 teaspoon of cloves, cinamon or any spice desired. Tie spice in muslin cloth; boil until currants are soft, add 1 pound of sugar, boil half hour. Very appetizing with cold meats.

Mrs. A. J. Crebbin.

Spiced Grapes.

Eight pounds of grapes, 5 pounds clarified sugar, 1½ pints vinegar, cloves, alspice, ground cinamon to taste. Pop the grapes out of the skins, and boil till you can rub through a collander to remove seed. Then put back on fire, with the skins, vinegar, sugar and spices, boil two hours.

Miss May Williams.

Unfermented Grape Wine.

Wash and pick grapes, put in porcelain kettle, let fruit heat until skins burst. Pour into cheese cloth bags and drip, then put juice back on stove; adding not quite ½ pint white sugar to 1 pint juice; boil rapidly 4 or 5 minutes; bottle and cork tightly, seal with wax or put into fruit jars.

MRS. ELLA EVERETT, Shubuta, Miss.

For Preserving Figs and Pears.

To 8 pounds of sugar add the strained juice of 2 lemons, and a table spoonful of stick cinnamon. Cut the rinds of the lemons, and put in the kettle with the other things; make the syrup with as little water as possible. When the syrup boils, put in 12 pounds of either figs or pears which have been through the lime process. Let boil until the fruit looks clear, and begins to sink, when it can be put in the jars.

MRS. J. B. WALKER.

Sour Orange Peeling Preserves.

Grate the yellow off of the orange, then peel it in four pieces, soak them two days in water (water must be changed every day to draw the bitter off); third day scald and drain well, then weigh them; use one pound of sugar to 1 pound of peeling, put the sugar in just enough water to cover it well, boil until a good syrup is obtained, then put in the peelings and cook until the syrup is quite thick.

MRS. M. C. D. LEHDE.

Miscellaneous.

Roast Turkey with Oyster Dressing.

After cleaning and thoroughly washing the turkey, pour boiling water all over it to plump it or make it tender. Rub it well with salt, then prepare dressing, as follows: about one loaf of stale bread, after it has soaked in hot water until soft, squeeze it dry. Chop one large onion, a small portion of celery, parsley and thyme. Half pound of sausage meat, add salt and pepper to season. Mix all together well. Put in a frying pan of hot lard and fry until brown, stirring constantly to prevent burning. When the dressing is done, stir in two or three dozen oysters chopped tolerably fine. Stuff the turkey with it and put what is left in the pan. Sift a little flour over the turkey to brown it, also one tablespoon lard. Fill the pan nearly full of hot water and baste the turkey with it, turning it occasionly until thoroughly cooked and brown.

Mrs. J. W. Billington.

Boiled Flour.

Tie tightly in a close linen cloth one pound of flour. After tying, moisten with water and dredge well with flour 'till a coating is formed to prevent the water entering the flour. Boil four or five hours and let the flour remain tied in the cloth until it is cold. It will be a hard, solid lump and is a substitute for arrow-root. Prepare by grating. Excellent in diarrhea or other bowel affections.

Diet for Infants.

Dissolve a piece of gelatine an inch square in half a gill of warm water; when dissolved, add a gill of milk; put on the fire, and when boiling add half a teaspoonful of arrow-root or boiled flour-ball. When sufficiently boiled, take off the fire and stir in two tablespoonsful of sweet cream. This may be given to very young infants; and as they grow older the food may be made stronger by using more milk or cream.   Mrs. Florence E. Russ

Cream Puffs.

One cup boiling water, ½ cup butter, put these on the stove, when boiling add one cup of flour, stir five minutes; put this off until nearly cold, then stir in one egg at a time until you get in five eggs. Soda size of a pea dissolved in teaspoonful cold water and put into the mixture. Have your tins hot. Bake twenty-five minutes and do not remove from tins until cold. Have oven very hot. Filling —One pint milk, one cup sugar, ½ cup flour, two eggs, beat yolks and flour together. Boil the milk and stir in mixture slowly, when it thickens take it off and let cool before putting in cakes. Flavor with Dixie vanilla extract.

Miss CLARA BILLINGTON.

Cake Icing.

To the white of 1 egg, add 9 heaped teaspoons of powdered sugar, 1 even teaspoon of cornstarch, and ¼ teaspoon of cream of tartar. Put all in together, and beat with a fork till too stiff to flow. The whites of 2 eggs and its accompanying ingredients will ice a good sized cake. Flavor to taste. If put on a hot cake, will not crumble off readily.

MRS. S. S. BOTHICK.

The Way to Make Good Coffee and Tea.

For making coffee or tea, *never* boil the water *more than three or four minutes* as most of its natural properties escape by evaporation, leaving very insipid liquid when boiled very long, which spoils the coffee or tea. Never use the water left in the tea-kettle over night, but have fresh boiled water always if you want good coffee or tea.

For tea, have an earthen or china pot, scald it out well and set on the stove, where it will dry and keep hot, when dry put in two teaspoonfuls of tea, let heat a minute or two and ten minutes before serving, pour in a pint of *fresh boiling water.*

Stuffed Peppers.

Select ½ dozed large green peppers, cut off the small ends and take out the seeds; then scald the peppers and drain them. Take any left-over meat, (veal preferred) and chop very fine, then chop up about two small tomatoes and half of a green pepper; ½ cup cold rice, season with salt and a little pepper; mix well and stuff the peppers. Set them in a pan half filled with water and a tablespoonfull of butter and a sprig of parsley; put in oven and bake until peppers are tender and brown, basting frequently. Miss L. KLOCKE.

Stuffed Eggs.

Boil 8 eggs hard, when cold peal and cut in half. Take out the yolks very carefully so as not to break the whites. Mash the yolks and mix with two teaspoons melted butter, one teaspoon mustard, three or four pieces pickled cucumbers chopped fine, salt and pepper to taste. Finely chopped ham, or celery seeds may be added. C. BILLINGTON.

Onion Soup.

Fry three medium sized onions in butter, a light brown color. Pour one pint rich, sweet milk into a granite boiler and place upon the stove; when it comes to a boil pour in the onions and season with butter, pepper and salt. Serve with toast. MRS. C. B. SHOLARS.

HOUSEHOLD HINTS.

Furniture Polish.

1 pint spirits of turpentine, ½ pint of sweet oil, 3 table-spoonsful of vinegar, 2 teaspoonsful flour. Excellent.

To Stiffen Collars.

A little gumarabic and common soda added to starch, gives extreme stiffness and gloss to shirt-bosoms and collars.

Home Made Yeast Powder.

1 pound of cream of tartar, ½ pound of soda, 1 pint of flour. Sift seven or eight times. Cover closely. Excellent.

Fat For Frying.

5 pounds pure cottonseed oil, 2 pounds beef suet. Cut the beef into small pieces, put into granite pot on the back of stove. Soon as the fat melts pour it off. Place cotton-seed oil in pot, then the beef suet. Cook together. When it has thoroughly boiled or reached 355° Fahrenheit, strain and put away.

To Clean Wall Paper.

To 1 pint of boiling water, add a full quart of flour and 2 tablespoonsful of ammonia, make into a stiff dough and rub down paper once.

Dip iron rust spots in tartaric acid and hang in the sun.

A sponge can be cleansed by soaking it a few hours in buttermilk.

Put a few apples into the box with your cake and they will keep it moist.

Hot water used in a sponge cake makes it white. Cold water produces a yellow cake.

A little borax or soda in the dish water makes the tinware brighter and is better than soap.

The juice of half a lemon in a tea cup of strong black coffee without sugar will often cure a sick headache.

Leather sachels may be cleaned with a sponge dipped in warm water in which a little oxalic acid has been dissolved.

Make a heavy line of tar about the paper on which the sugar bowl stands, if you are troubled with ants and they will never cross the tar line.

In making cake if you have the yolks left and do not care to use them right away, cover them with fresh water and they will keep for three days.

Turpentine will drive away ants and roaches if sprinkled about shelves and closets. A teaspoonful in a pail of warm water cleans paint excellently. A little in the boiler on washing day whitens the clothes.

Nothing has proved to be so great a preservative of leather as castor oil, at the same time keeping the leather silky and supple. That is because the oil does not soak into the leather, nor permit the water to do so, and preserves the natural condition and life of the leather. As a preservative next in value is castor oil and neatfoot, half and half mixed.

Weights and Measures.

The following table of weights and measures will be useful, and they have the merit of being correct:

Butter the size of an egg—2 ounces.

Butter the size of a walnut—1 ounce.

One solid pint of chopped meat—1 pound.

Eight or ten eggs—1 pound.

One coffee cupful of butter, pressed down—$\frac{1}{2}$ pound.

Four teaspoonsful—1 tablespoonsful liquid.

One tablespoonful of soft butter, well rounded—1 ounce.

Four tablespoonsful, or half a gill—1 wine glass.

Two coffee cupfuls—1 pint.

Two pints—1 quart.

Four quarts—1 gallon.

Two tablespoonfuls liquid—1 ounce.

One tablespoonful of salt—1 ounce.

Sixteen ounces—1 pound, or a pint of liquid.

One rounded tablespoonful of flour—$\frac{1}{2}$ ounce.

Three cups of corn meal—1 pound.

Four coffee cupfuls of sifted flour—1 pound.

One quart of unsifted flour—1 pound.

One pint of granulated sugar—1 pound.

Two coffee cupfuls of powdered sugar—1 pound.

One pint of brown sugar—thirteen ounces.

Two and a half cups of powdered sugar—1 pound.

INDEX.

www.ingramcontent.com/pod-product-compliance
Lightning Source LLC
Chambersburg PA
CBHW021408090426
42742CB00009B/1064